INDIANS

Volume 3

Oregon Country Series

Rick Steber

Illustrations by Don Gray

NOTE

INDIANS is the third book in an Oregon Country Series. Each volume contains stories written by Rick Steber which first appeared in his syndicated newspaper column, "Oregon Country".

Indians
Volume 3
Oregon Country Series

First Printing June 1987

Bonanza Publications, Ltd.
Box 204
Prineville, Oregon 97754

INTRODUCTION

Stone age people from Siberia are believed to have crossed on an ice bridge to North America between 35,000 and 100,000 years ago. These aboriginals withstood the latter stages of an ice age, catastrophic floods and volcanic eruptions.

Approximately 100,000 Indians lived in the Oregon Country before the coming of the white-skinned men. The natives had no immunity to the white man's plagues and fell victim to smallpox, fever and ague, tuberculosis, measles and venereal disease. The death rate among the Chinook tribe at the mouth of the Columbia River reached 95%. Entire villages were exterminated.

Within a single generation the native population was reduced to fewer than 15,000 people. The survivors were spread over a large territory and the whites who came for fur, gold and land took what they wanted. The Indians could offer little resistance.

As this new race flooded the Oregon Country, the Indians were herded onto reservations. When their reservation land was found to be rich in timber, minerals and farm ground, they were pushed onto the poorest land. Those who chose to fight were killed or exiled to the Oklahoma Territory. The Indian way of life was doomed.

MOUNTAIN FEVER

It was called mountain fever and meant suffering, agony and death for the native population. In three years, from 1829 to 1832, an estimated 30,000 Indians died from it in the Oregon Country.

Some Indians claimed this vial of pestilence was uncorked by the white trappers and traders. Others felt that the plowing of fields at Fort Vancouver had touched off the pandemic.

At the village of Wakanassi, six miles from Fort Vancouver, the dead were heaped in a ghastly open tomb six feet deep and 160 feet long. Within three weeks of the first outbreak of sickness the tribe, which had once boasted 500 warriors, was reduced to Chief Kesano and six survivors.

David McLoughlin, son of Doctor John McLoughlin, told of the horrible desolation caused by the mountain fever, stating many years later: "Once there were villages along the Columbia all the way from the sea to the Cascades. All these plains were covered with tepees and warriors came dashing down these hills. Where are they now? A typhoid malaria came shortly after the first plowing of fields at Fort Vancouver and the Indians died by the hundreds and by the thousands. A quietness came over the land. No more Indian shouts and halloos and games of ball. No more Indians came up to Fort Vancouver with furs. There was a stench from all the waters, and buzzards hovered in the sky. The bones were corded up like wood and burned in great funeral pyres. The streams were filled with corpses that floated out to sea, for always in the fever the natives leaped into the cold Columbia and never lived to reach shore. They died in the water. The Oregon Country was depopulated."

WHITMAN MASSACRE

Mrs. James Cason was a small girl in 1847. She lived with her father in one of the six adobe huts on the Whitman Mission. On the afternoon of November 29 the Cayuse Indians went on the warpath and the young girl was left a homeless orphan.

She recalled, "I was washing dishes when I heard the report of a gun. That was the shot that killed Gilliam, the tailor. The Indians stood in the doorway and shot him. And as the horrible work was going on outside I and some others went upstairs where we could look from a window and see part of the conflict."

The children watched as Doctor Whitman was called to the door and tomahawked. Fourteen people, including Doctor Whitman, his wife Narcissa and Mrs. Cason's father were killed. The Indians rounded up the others, 53 women and children, and held them as hostages.

As soon as Peter Skene Ogden, chief factor of the Hudson's Bay Company post at Fort Vancouver, learned of the massacre he immediately led a company of men to Fort Walla Walla. On December 29 he was able to win the release of the captives by paying a ransom of $400 worth of blankets, shirts, tobacco, guns and ammunition.

Volunteers were organized and kept the Cayuse on the run until the spring of 1850. The survivors, on the verge of starvation, gave up five Indians who they claimed had taken part in the massacre. Governor Joseph Lane, with an escort consisting of a lieutenant and ten men from the rifle regiment, brought the five to Oregon City. A trial was held, a verdict of guilty returned and on the 3rd of June, 1850, the five Indians were hung.

EYES OF TIME

Petowya, daughter of Tomatoppo, chief of the Umatillas, witnessed the coming of Lewis and Clark. The expedition visited her village on the bank of the Umatilla River on the return trip. It was many years before trappers and traders began wandering through the country. Petowya listened to their fantastic stories of cities on the far side of the great mountains. She did not always believe them. Trappers were known to exaggerate.

One day Petowya was sitting on the bank of the Umatilla River when she noticed a strange sight. Upon investigating, she discovered wagons with canvas covers being driven down the face of a long hill. Every fall after that, as regular as the migrating geese, more wagons passed through the land of the Umatillas.

White men built a town on the south bank of the Columbia River and called it Umatilla. They traveled up and down the river in steamboats. They mined for gold in the mountains, cut the timber and made homes. They plowed the rolling hills and planted wheat.

The Lewis and Clark Exposition, marking the 100th anniversary of the expedition, was scheduled to be held in Portland in 1905. One of the guests invited to attend and tell of actually having met Lewis and Clark was Petowya. But the Indian woman who had witnessed so much history died of old age. She was 113 years old.

AFTER THE WAR

The war of the Lava Beds had been lost and the Modoc Indians were exiled to the Quapaw Reservation in the Oklahoma Indian Territory. The spring of 1874 a correspondent for the *St. Louis Dispatch* visited the Modocs at their barracks.

He wrote of his meeting with the head chief, Scarface Charley: "The desire was expressed to witness the skill of the Modocs with the bow and arrow. Scarface issued some orders in his native tongue, and in less than a minute thirty bucks appeared upon the scene, armed with bows and arrows and dressed in the most fantastic garbs imaginable; one had on buckskin leggins and a lady's skirt of which he was evidently proud, another had nothing on but a pair of army pants.

"To show off their bows, an inch-thick pine board was propped up and one of the Modocs stepped off 25 paces. His arrow was a plain wooden shaft. But the bow was powerful enough to drive the shaft through the pine board.

"Everything being ready for a trial of skill, a twig was split and stuck in the ground and I was requested to donate a nickel which was put on top of the twig. At a distance of 25 yards the contestants arranged themselves in a line. The shooting was extraordinarily accurate. Each time the stick was hit the man responsible went running to claim the money and I would dig again in my pocket for more change."

THE SWAN

E-tsa-wis-no was approaching manhood. One day his father walked him to the edge of the Nez Perce camp and told him, "You are about to become a man. You must journey into the mountains. The Great Spirit, taking the form of a bird or animal, will speak to you of the moon and the sun and the stars. Listen. Follow your Weyekin."

The Weyekin, spirit ally, did not come quickly. E-tsa-wis-no stayed in a camp beside a high mountain lake and finally, after ten days of fasting, the Great Spirit appeared in dazzling moonlight as an elegant white swan. The swan landed on the lake and swam to E-tsa-wis-no, spoke to him, saying, "I am your Weyekin. I will lead you. Watch. Study. Know all there is to know about the swan. And when you are ready you shall be a swan. You shall fly."

E-tsa-wis-no recognized this to be a very powerful sign and he gave himself fully to the Great Spirit. He watched and studied and learned.

Seasons changed. Five times the cycle of life was repeated before the young man was seen again by members of his tribe. He was seen as he passed overhead, flying in a formation of swans. He was a swan with feathered wings but he had retained the body of a man. And every year after, he was observed flying south in the fall and north in the spring.

6

SELLING THE VALLEY

The United States and Great Britain jointly occupied the Northwest Indian lands until 1846 when a treaty established the 49th parallel as the boundary. Two years later the Oregon Territory was created.

It was not until 1855 that the United States government sought a treaty with the Indians for sole ownership of the Willamette Valley. Pioneers, in ever increasing numbers, were laying claim to the rich farm land and the government felt it imperative that title be clearly established.

Indian Superintendent Joel Palmer entered into treaty negotiations with the Calapooia nation which controlled most of the large valley. Over a seventeen-day period he rode horseback from village to village securing the signature of 46 chiefs and subchiefs of the various bands. With a single mark or an X beside their names, the Indians agreed to cede 1,460 square miles of fertile land.

For relinquishing title they received a small reservation allowing about 40 acres per family and the government's promise to supply them with $155,000 worth of goods, payable over a 20-year period at the discretion of the President. An industrial school was to be established and a school teacher was to be supplied as well as a blacksmith and a superintendent of farming operations.

Joel Palmer, in a letter to General Lane, a delegate in Congress, wrote: "No one will for a moment pretend that the amount proposed to be paid (to the Confederated Bands of the Willamette Valley) is any consideration, comparatively speaking, for their country."

DANGEROUS JOURNEY

The summer afternoon was warm and the canyon full of the sound of Hurricane Creek as it tumbled from the high mountains to the Wallowa Valley below. On a bench in the canyon tepees surrounded a fire, their whiteness standing out starkly from the dark green forest. Indian children were playing a stick game. A young girl stooped to add a few chunks of wood to the fire.

The tranquility of the Nez Perce camp was abruptly altered by a string of war whoops. A raiding party of Bannocks attacked, launching a barrage of arrows. They stole the young girl tending the fire and carried her far to the south, to their high desert homeland.

All the time the girl was held as a slave she dreamed of the beautiful Wallowa Valley. Seasons melted one into another. Finally the girl was able to escape.

One night those in the Nez Perce camp were shocked to see a vision of the young girl as she appeared in the firelight. But this was not a vision. Still, it was unthinkable anyone so young could escape the Bannocks, elude the search party and cross hundreds of miles of rugged country.

The girl explained. A white wolf had led her across the desert and through the mountains. Once it doubled back and killed a mountain lion in a savage fight. The white wolf brought her all the way to the edge of camp, then disappeared.

From that day forward the girl was known as Wet-koo-wisha, which translates to, "One Who Returns From Dangerous Journey".

STOUT HEART

The pioneering Pritchard family took an isolated homestead along the Rogue River. Their log cabin sat back in the timber at the head of a long, open meadow.

One hot summer afternoon they noticed smoke coming from the direction of their nearest neighbor and knew the local Indians, who had been threatening hostility, had gone on the warpath.

The Pritchard family barricaded themselves inside the cabin. The first night passed uneventfully but in the light of morning Molly Pritchard noticed shadows slinking from tree to tree. She called to her husband and instructed the children to crawl under the bed and stay there.

A war party of at least one hundred Indians attacked the cabin. Mr. Pritchard was killed in the initial volley. Without a moment of grieving Molly scooped up the rifle, reloaded and took her place at the open window. She fired and reloaded again and again.

The battle, with the Indians surging forward and retreating, continued all that day. Sometimes Molly would slump to the floor, momentarily overcome by the tragedy and the circumstances; but each time the wild howls of the Indians and the cries of her own children would revive her.

Late in the afternoon a string of gunshots was heard at the far end of the meadow; a few minutes later men's voices were audible. A party of settlers had come to the rescue. They freed Molly and her children from the house and located the bodies of 20 Indians killed by the stout-hearted woman.

MEMALOOSE ISLAND

Victor Trevitt, keeper of the Mt. Hood Saloon and a prominent pioneer in The Dalles, fought in the Cayuse Indian War of 1848 and in the Yakima Indian War of 1855; but in the ensuing years he changed his opinion of the red man.

"I have but one desire after I die," requested Trevitt, "to be laid away on Memaloose Island with the Indians. They are more honest than the whites. In resurrection I will take my chances with the Indians. I wouldn't have any chance to get into the white man's heaven, anyway. Maybe I can slip in with the Indians."

Memaloose Island, in the Columbia River below The Dalles, had been an Indian burial ground from time immemorial. The rocky island was covered with bleached bones of the deceased and items they might need in the spirit world: bows and arrows, knives, blankets, trinkets and guns. This land was sacred to the Indian.

After Trevitt's death in 1883, in keeping with his last request, arrangements were made to intern him on Memaloose Island. The Masons, of which Trevitt was a life-long member, conducted services and a large congregation accompanied the casket on the steamer *Hassalo* to Memaloose Island. On the high point a brick vault had been prepared for the reception of the remains. The casket was lowered, the vault sealed and a fourteen-foot tall slab of marble erected.

The Indians considered this an infringement on their sacred ground. Never again did they use Memaloose Island. Today, all that remains is the marble slab marking the final resting spot of Victor Trevitt.

CAYUSE

According to Indian legend the horse was brought to the Oregon Country by a member of the Walla Walla tribe, a shaman who was given the gift of vision by the Great Spirit.

This shaman had a re-occurring dream. He told his fellow tribesmen, "I have a vision of an animal. It looks like an elk without horns. It has long hair on its neck and rump. And it carries a man dressed in black on its back. I see this far to the south."

"You must go. Bring this animal to us," the chief informed him. The following morning the shaman began his journey traveling south, always south. Each night the vision grew more vivid.

One day a crow appeared, made tight circles around the Indian and then flew south. The bird repeated this strange behavior. The shaman understood he was to follow.

At last, suffering from exhaustion and lack of water, the Indian collapsed in the shade of a tall cactus. When he awoke he spoke the words, "I have arrived." In the distance he recognized his vision, a man dressed in black riding an elk-like animal.

The Indian killed the man, a padre, and stole the animal. He escaped north to the land of the Walla Wallas where the horse, a bred mare, foaled. A male colt was born. From this beginning came the Indian horse, the Cayuse.

Grey

13

THE PLAN

It used to be said that the only good Indian was a dead Indian. And there were some white men who made sure there were only "good Indians". If they caught an Indian alone, he was used for target practice.

Of course, this practice led to bad feelings, reprisals and more bloodshed. One such reprisal was the killing of Martin Angel. He was returning to his homestead from the settlement of Jacksonville when he was shot in the back by Indians.

Angel's death set off a wave of hostile sentiment among the miners and homesteaders and a group of volunteers was quickly organized. They rode directly to the nearest Indian village but the Indians had pulled out. They followed the trail until night overtook them and they were forced to set camp. The Indians kept going, fleeing onward into the mountains.

With the light of a new day the volunteers gave chase, climbing ever higher. At one point, crossing a bald face of loose shale, the mule carrying ammunition lost its footing, rolled over and over and was finally dashed against the boulders lining Applegate River.

The volunteers continued and were able to overtake a group of stragglers, a few squaws and one old blind man. They realized they would never catch the able-bodied and so returned to Jacksonville with their prisoners, hoping that the braves would come in on their own to free their women. But they never did. After feeding the prisoners for half the winter the citizens of Jacksonville gave up on the plan and turned them loose.

BILLY CHINOOK

Billy Chinook was an Indian who accepted the white man. While others of his race fought to put distance between themselves and the invaders, Billy Chinook was baptized into Christianity. He was filled with an overwhelming desire to know everything about the white man and his ways.

When explorer John C. Fremont reached Celilo Falls on the Columbia River, Billy Chinook was there to greet him. Fremont was impressed with the Indian and hired him to assist Kit Carson as a scout for the expedition. Billy Chinook led the way through familiar country south to California where they made a dangerous mid-winter crossing of the Sierra Nevada mountains.

From California Billy Chinook traveled to the east coast and enrolled in Columbia College to learn to speak, write and read the white man's language. He came west by covered wagon to California. Within a few years he became disenchanted with the white man's civilization and returned home to the Columbia River and resumed his Indian ways.

In 1855 when the Wasco tribe was called upon to sign a peace treaty with the United States, it was Billy Chinook who studied the terms and explained the treaty to his tribe. He said the Indian would preserve the right to fish the Columbia River "until the salmon come no more". Billy Chinook never envisioned the day the white man would block the great river with dams and stop the salmon from running.

The body of Billy Chinook lies for eternity in the Warm Springs cemetery beneath a tombstone which reads: "A faithful and true friend of the white men, William Chinook, died at the age of 63".

INDIAN GAMBLING

Indians loved games of chance and sometimes all a gambler's worldly possessions, including wives, might be added to the pot. Losses were accepted without complaint or self-pity.

In the bone game, a polished bone was held by one man while an opponent was challenged to guess which hand held the bone. Stick counters were passed from the loser to the winner. Any number of persons could wager during a game and players could be replaced by anyone who was thought to hold the most supernatural power, or luck, at that particular time. Chanting, dancing and calling upon the spirits were permissible. One game might last for days.

Occasionally a blind person would be chosen to manipulate the hiding of the bone. The blind were usually quicker and more deceptive with their hands and under intense stares from the other side, they could maintain better poker faces.

Indian women developed their own forms of gambling. By carving various marks they fashioned casting bones similar to dice. The combination of marked or unmarked sides determined the winner.

All types of bone were used, but Indians favored certain animals because they believed the Gods gave those animals special powers. One Klamath legend relates that during a battle a cavalry soldier was killed and his forearms taken by a warrior to use for gambling sticks. But the gods were displeased and sent the ghost of the soldier to haunt the Indian.

THE ALL-SEEING EYE

The sun dropped into the notch carved by the Columbia River and the Indians lamented, mourning the loss of heat and light. They prayed to the Sun; beseeched his wife, the Moon, and his children, the Stars, to send him back to Earth.

In the morning, as the eastern sky began to color, the Indians rejoiced and made themselves ready with purification baths. With the sun flickering gold on the horizon, they ran to the top of a hill, sang and danced.

Sun worshipping was in direct conflict with Christianity and when homesteaders settled the Columbia river valley, there was a great deal of discussion concerning the pagan religion of the local Indians. It was rumored that, like the sun-worshipping Aztecs of Mexico, these Indians offered human sacrifices on a stone altar.

Within a single generation the Columbia River sun worshippers disappeared. They left behind markings on the hard basalt cliffs, nothing more. The markings provide a window to the past, to an interesting and strange sect. One depicts the stick figure of man encircled in a blazing sun. In another, the sun is at the center of a number of concentric rings. Some markings show the sun with human characteristics: mouth, nose, eyes and hair.

One of the best examples of the pagan worshippers' art is the Umatilla stone. It was found along the Columbia River and contains a carving of the sun's all-seeing eye. It was removed and transferred to Portland where today it guards the morning side of City Hall.

COYOTE

According to a San Poil Indian legend: "In the beginning of time, Coyote had great power. He said to himself, 'I have such power, why remain in seclusion?' He began to travel down the Columbia River. Along the way he met Sparrow wearing a beaded warbonnet. Coyote coveted the bonnet. He killed Sparrow, put on the bonnet and continued his journey, staying close to the water so he could admire his own reflection.

"As Coyote walked, he heard Grouse children and thought they mocked him so he put pitch over their eyes to blind them. In retaliation Grouse mother boomed at him and frightened Coyote so that he fell off a high bluff into the river. During the fall Coyote changed himself into a basket so he would fall more lightly.

"Downstream there were two women who had built a dam to hold back the salmon. They found the pretty basket, took it to camp and used it to store smoked salmon. But the salmon mysteriously vanished. The women realized the basket was enchanted and threw it into the fire. But as the flames consumed it a boy emerged from the smoke and the women, feeling motherly, adopted him.

"One evening the women returned from berry picking to find the boy had transformed himself into Coyote and had broken down the dam. Coyote changed one of the women into a snipe and the other into a killdeer. Then Coyote began following the salmon upstream. At those villages where the maidens welcomed him, he gave salmon to them as gifts. But at those villages where the maidens rejected him, he kept the salmon away."

That is the Indian version of how waterfalls were created.

THE WORLD BEYOND

The first white men to the Northwest introduced the small-pox virus and the native population, without natural immunity to the disease, died by the thousands.

One old Indian from a village along the Columbia River felt the smallpox fever come on him. He knew the fever would rage for a few days and his skin would erupt with open sores. After agonizing for a week or two, he would die. He had seen the terrible suffering among his people all too many times. He gathered his few belongings and voluntarily banished himself from camp.

It was the custom of his tribe to bury the dead; they believed that only by burial was one's soul set free. The old man picked out a spot overlooking the river and dug his own grave. He fashioned a wood frame over the hole and strung his blanket across the top. He lay down, secure in the knowledge that after he died the blanket would eventually rot and his body would fall into the grave.

He waited patiently for the disease to consume him. Instead, over the course of several days, the fever subsided. His breathing came easier and his sight, which had become hazy, cleared.

At long last he concluded he was not going to die. He rose from his deathbed and return to his people. But the invisible enemy had destroyed his tribe. Bodies were strewn about the village. The old man began the grim task of burying the dead so that their spirits would be set free to journey to the world beyond.

INDIAN TOBACCO

Indian men used to sit around campfires smoking. They called their tobacco kinnikinnick (pronounced ka-nick-ka-nick) and obtained it from bearberry plants or the innerbark of the red willow.

Bearberry is native to the coast and the mountainous regions of the Oregon Country. It grows in a spreading mat characterized by inconspicuous white flowers and scarlet berries about the size of small cherries.

Early-day botanist David Douglas described encountering Indian tobacco in the fall of 1825. He wrote: "I first saw a single plant of tobacco in the hand of an Indian at the Great Falls on the Columbia (Celilo), but though I offered two ounces of manufactured tobacco, an enormous remuneration, he would on no account part with it. The Nicotiana is never sowed by the Indians near the villages lest it should be pulled and used before it comes to perfect maturity; they select for its cultivation an open place in the wood where they burn a dead tree or stump and, strewing the ashes over the ground, plant tobacco there. Fortunately, I happened to detect one of these little plantations and supplied myself, without delay of immediate stipulations for payment, with both specimens for drying and seed. The owner, whom I shortly met, seeing the prize under my arm appeared much displeased, but was propitiated with a present of European tobacco, and becoming good friends with me, gave the above description of its culture, saying that wood ashes invariably made it grow very large."

FIRE HUNT

Before the coming of the white man the Indians of the Willamette Valley would meet in a friendly gathering to hunt meat for the coming winter.

The hunt began with men stationed several hundred yards apart in a huge circle. At the first sign of dawn the Indians set fire to the grass. By afternoon the wild animals were fleeing from the flames toward the center of the great circle.

Late in the day a handful of the best hunters entered the ring of fire. They selected the animals to kill, always sparing the biggest and strongest, the females, and the young. Only the old and the injured were harvested. As the flames advanced they herded the remaining animals into marshes where they would escape the fire.

The Indian practice of hunting with fire kept the center of the Willamette Valley free of brush and timber. And the selective killing of the inferior animals guaranteed survival of the breeding stock and assured there would always be an adequate supply of meat going into winter.

WARNING

On the coast of the Oregon Country lived the Makahs, to the south were the Quillayutes. They were warring nations and often conducted raids, killing each other and stealing young girls for slaves.

Between these fierce enemies was the village of the Ozette tribe. They maintained neutrality even though their unwillingness to join as an ally caused resentment from both neighbors. As a result the Makahs and Quillayutes would often stop at the Ozette village, celebrating victory or making up for defeat by killing a few Ozettes.

Once a big storm forced a war party of Quillayutes to land near the Ozette village. The warriors were welcomed and invited to a great celebration where they feasted and were entertained with drumming and dancing. The fires were built up. The visitors became sleepy.

While the Quillayutes slept the Ozette warriors systematically killed them, 47 in all. They cut off their heads and placed them on tall poles on the beach. There they remained as a macabre warning to all who traveled the coast.

SACRIFICE

It was tradition among some Indian tribes that when their chief died, a young slave girl be sacrificed. Doctor John McLoughlin, the father of Oregon, put a stop to this practice; but in 1844, with the death of Chief Cleek-a-tuck, the tradition was revived.

A young slave girl was selected, taken to the sweathouse and held under guard. The tribal leaders counciled, discussed the ceremony and decided the girl should have her hands and feet bound and be placed in an elevated canoe with the body of Chief Cleek-a-tuck. If she did not die from exposure within three days she would be killed.

The slave girl overheard her captors plotting the sacrifice. As they led her from the sweathouse she escaped, ran to the river, leaped in and swam to the far side to where a white man and his wife had built a cabin. The man was away but his wife was home. She took in the Indian girl.

"Give us girl!" demanded the warriors, but the woman refused. She brandished a rifle and vowed, "I will not. She is not your property. You are trespassing. Leave."

She spoke with such conviction the warriors backed away. They recrossed the Clackamas River to their village. When Doctor McLoughlin learned of their intentions to revive slave sacrifice he punished those responsible. The slave girl stayed with the settlers and was raised as their child.

HUNTING

The Indians of the Oregon Country were masters of hunting. Their livelihood depended on their skill.

Men were the principal hunters. They used a variety of techniques including covered pitfalls, snares made from bent saplings that jerked an animal into the air, and deadfalls (a heavy rock or log balanced over a bait and triggered to fall when an animal disturbed the bait).

Big game animals were hunted with bow and arrow. The bows were made of yew, oak or juniper with a twisted sinew string. The arrows were fashioned from cedar or hardwood and tipped with sharp obsidian.

Antelope were hunted on the high desert, deer and elk in the mountains. Occasionally an Indian would track down and kill a bear for the glory of killing such a powerful animal. All parts of an animal were used: teeth and claws for decoration, fur for clothing, antlers for tools, meat for food, and the leftovers to feed the dogs or bait traps.

Birds were hunted. During mating season the sage grouse was preoccupied with its dancing ritual and could be clubbed. Ducks and geese were attracted by decoys, feathered skins stuffed with tule reeds. Small animals like rabbits, squirrels and groundhogs were also hunted. And during times of famine lizards and even insects, ants and grasshoppers, were used as a food source.

STICK WOMAN

The year was 1877. Chief Joseph and his Nez Perce tribe were retreating toward Canada. At Big Hole, Montana, the Indians were attacked by U.S. Army regulars. One of the first to be captured was a woman named To-ka-map-map-e. Her hands were tied and she was set behind a soldier on a horse and taken away from the front to be interrogated.

As they neared the military camp To-ka-map-map-e was able to free her hands and work the soldier's knife from its sheath. He never knew, only felt the sharp bite of the metal and the burning sensation in the small of his back. He rolled out of the saddle and the Indian woman took the reins. She rode directly through the battle to Chief Joseph, reported all she had seen in the Army camp, gave numbers and positions of the troops.

In the battle, 31 soldiers were killed and 38 were seriously wounded. But the Nez Perce lost 89 warriors and the war. They were banished to the Indian Territory in Oklahoma.

Eventually To-ka-map-map-e escaped and returned to Oregon. She lived to be a very old woman. But instead of being known as a survivor of the Nez Perce retreat and a participant in the battle of Big Hole, she was most known because of a photograph. The widely-circulated photograph showed a defeated old woman carrying an enormous load of branches on her bowed back. It was simply titled, "Stick Woman".

26

REPAYING KINDNESS

White settlers arrived in the Umpqua valley and established a small settlement. Ten miles away was an Indian village that became ravaged by disease.

The winter of 1841 was severe and this added to the Indians' woes. At last a delegation was dispatched to the settlement. They described the horrible scene at their camp; brothers, sisters, mothers and fathers all dead or dying. They begged for help.

Only three white men answered the call. They traveled to the Indian village and found the natives trying to cure their sickness by taking sweatbaths and then leaping into the cold water of the Umpqua.

The men stayed with the Indians for several weeks, tending fires, comforting the sick and burying the dead. Eventually the epidemic ran its course. Those who remained steadily grew stronger. The men returned to hunting and fishing. The women cooked and gathered wood for the fires. The three white men were no longer needed. They returned to the settlement.

One dark night a band of renegades slipped into the settlement. They drove away all the animals, except for the stock of the three men who had come to the aid of the Indians. They lost nothing.

28

RENEGADE

At the turn of this century there was an old Indian who roamed the high desert near where the states of Oregon, Idaho and Nevada meet. The buckaroos who worked around those parts knew him by his white man's name -- Jim.

Jim made the rounds from one cow camp to the next, always timing his arrival to coincide with a meal. After his belly was full he departed. He never caused trouble and rarely spoke unless addressed directly.

It was rumored that Jim had a dark past; that he had been involved in the Bannock Indian War and as a blood-thirsty sub-chief he had led the massacre and scalping of a detachment of soldiers and the kidnapping of a white woman.

One time a buckaroo asked Jim, "You savvy the fight you had with the soldiers?"

"I savvy," grunted the Indian.

"You savvy what you done with the white woman?"

"No savvy," replied Jim with an icy glare that repelled further questions. That short exchange was the only time Jim ever addressed the matter of the massacre and the kidnapping.

One winter Jim was caught between ranches in a blizzard. His body was found several weeks later wrapped in a blanket, facing east.

PAIUTES

The Paiute tribe occupied the most desolate stretches of the high desert. They lived in bands of ten to forty families and set lodges on familiar camp sites, moving nomadically with the changing seasons.

The Paiutes harvested the salmon and steelhead that ran up the rivers to spawn. They gathered pine nuts and pinon pine nuts, grinding them with a mortar to make flour. What the buffalo was to the Sioux, the rabbit was to the Paiute; they ate the meat fresh, smoke-cured what was extra, and sewed the hides together for clothing and blankets. In early spring they caught ground squirrels emerging from winter hibernation by pouring water in their holes to force the animals to the surface. Annual mud hen drives were held in tule marshes where the birds were corralled and clubbed. The diet of the Paiutes depended on the generosity of Mother Nature. Sometimes they were reduced to eating ants.

The Paiutes were deeply religious. They prayed and offered sacrifices to the Sun God and the Rain God and asked the Great Spirit to allow the fish to run in the rivers. When a member of the tribe died, the others would gather and wail while the deceased and all earthly possessions were placed on a pyre of sage and burned.

Today members of the Paiute tribe remain tied to the old ways. Some modern Indians run away from whirlwinds, believing they are the breath of an evil spirit and that being caught in a dust devil causes instant death.

WHITE STALLION

Each fall the Blackfeet Indians crossed the Rocky Mountains to hunt buffalo, trade and gamble with the Plains Indians. For many years a white stallion in their possession won all the horse races and the Blackfeet accumulated wealth and prestige because of him.

But one year a Crow boy, hoping to prove his manhood, vowed to steal the wonderful horse. On a moonless night he approached the camp of the Blackfeet, crawled through tall grass to a vantage point on a hill overlooking the camp. He watched as the stallion was paraded in the firelight and then led inside a tepee. Four warriors were posted as guards and the flap was tied shut.

He waited until the fire was burning low before he advanced slowly, silently. Several times he stepped over sleeping dogs. At last he reached the tepee that concealed the stallion. In the dim light he noticed a travois and without making a sound he leaned it against the tepee. He climbed it like a ladder and peered down through the smoke hole. He could see the horse and his four guards.

Knowing what he must do, he acted quickly. Like a rock he dropped through the hole and landed squarely onto the back of the stallion. All in the same motion he dug his heels into the horse's ribs and swung his knife in a quick arc, cutting the skin wall. The magnificent white horse jumped through the opening and was swallowed by the blackness of the night.

PROUD BE INDIAN

Kanina was a Walla Walla Indian and in 1898 he reflected upon the coming of the white man and the changes which had come over the land.

"I 80 years old. Pretty near last of old tribe. Chief Peo dead. Howlish Wampo dead. Strong Saddle Blanket here no more.

"Reservation land raise good wheat. Me no care farm. Rent land wheat trader, $4 acre, cash money. Him work. I sit play poker. Earth is mother, have no step-mother. Earth look out us Indians.

"Pendleton. Kind of white man start town us Indians, so close reservation. Bring us railroad, ice cream, drug store, good ginger cookie.

"Horse, first time, scarce reservation. Doubt have 10,000 head. Measure wealth horse. I trade cayuse. White man buy. Him kill horse. Eat horse. No good eat horse.

"White man say I no good talk. Forget I graduate Wild Horse Academy Music. I know enough wear blanket. Blanket keep out cold. Blanket keep out heat too.

"Indian prosper under white man. Look Charlie Blackhawk. Him have many row tack on vest. Make shiny mark sun. May be good other thing too.

"I Indian. Smell sagebrush smoke. Ride horse good. Never go bald. Never be white man. Proud be Indian."

WAR BONNET

Back in 1903 Enos Cambell was a fourteen-year-old boy setting out on an adventure. He departed St. Louis aboard a rundown saddle horse and managed to nurse it to Oregon.

Enos recalled, "For a while I worked on a farm in the Willamette Valley but I was bit by the wander bug. I hopped a freight in Portland and headed north. Went as far north as I could get, Canada, and took off on foot to see what was over the next range of mountains.

"I walked for the better part of two weeks before coming across a log cabin sitting at the edge of a beaver pond. It was as beautiful and peaceful a spot as can be found in this world.

"At first I thought the place deserted. There wasn't a fire in the stove. But on closer inspection I found an old Indian man lying on a bunk on the dirt floor. He had busted a leg and by the time I found him, gangrene had set in. He was pretty close to dying.

"I started a fire. Made a broth with some meat I had shot the day before and helped the poor fellow eat. The soup seemed to revive him. He told me, in a voice barely above a whisper, that he was half Indian and half French-Canadian. Said he had been at the battle of Little Big Horn, had helped kill Custer, that after the massacre he had run away, come to Canada, built the cabin and lived in it ever since.

"He didn't last long. Before he died he told me about his war bonnet, said it was in a trunk under the bed and told me to take it.

"I buried him. And I found the war bonnet where he said it was. It had 28 eagle feathers and each fit into a concho made from a U.S. cavalry button.

"I packed that bonnet around with me for years but one day a fellow offered me fifty bucks for it. I was broke so I sold it."

EVIL CHIEF

Many moons ago the man-people lived in the valley and the animals lived in the mountains. They were brothers and spoke the same language.

An evil chief took control of the man-people. He claimed he was greater than Tomanous (the Great Spirit) and began killing animals that would not obey his command.

The animals were very frightened and called Tomanous to council. The Great Spirit instructed them to leave and go east of the mountains. They all departed except Wildcat who moved into camp with the evil chief.

When the evil chief realized the animals, birds and fish had gone, he was angry and ordered Wildcat to leave his fire; but Wildcat refused, humped his back and spit in the air. This infuriated the evil chief and he grabbed Wildcat by the scruff of his neck and held him over the fire. Over the wailing of Wildcat he announced, "From this day forward Wildcat shall have no tail."

Then Tomanous spoke, asking the evil chief, "Why you burn off Wildcat tail?"

"Because Wildcat only animal left and he want to be chief," came the answer.

"Fool," cried Tomanous. "He was your only friend and now I drive Wildcat from this land." And with that pronouncement, a black cloud rolled from the mountains and fire fell like rain. Thunder shook the ground. Tomanous lifted the evil chief high above the earth, threw him in a hole in the ground and covered the hole with deep blue water.

This is the Indian legend describing the creation of Crater Lake. Even today some Indians refuse to visit the lake because they carry the belief that the spirit of the evil chief resides there.

INDIAN WAR

Harrison Brunk and his wife had taken a land claim west of the small settlement of Salem, Oregon. One day, while Harrison was out farming, there came a sharp rap. Mrs. Brunk opened the cabin door and an Indian pushed past her, stumbled into the kitchen and plopped onto a chair.

Mrs. Brunk recognized the Indian as Patac, chief of the Calapooia tribe. He had always been friendly but this day his face was covered with war paint and he was holding his side. Blood oozed between his fingers.

Patac made sign, rubbing his stomach and licking his lips, indicating that he wanted something to eat. Mrs. Brunk gave him bread and milk. While the Indian ate, dipping chunks of bread in the milk and gulping them down, a pool of blood formed on the floor around his chair.

Mrs. Brunk, afraid the chief might bleed to death in her kitchen, asked in jargon how he had been injured. Patac answered that a war party of Klickitats had invaded the Willamette Valley and attacked the Calapooia village. He reassured the woman, "Klickitat lose little blood and die. Calapooia loose much blood, never die."

At last the wounded chief rose from the table and shuffled off toward the battlefield. Late that afternoon he returned to announce the Calapooias had won and to invite the Brunks to the celebration. That night the couple watched the Calapooias dance around a pole from which hung the head of the defeated chief.

TRAIL OF TEARS

The Reverend H.K. Hines, a Methodist missionary, arrived in the Umpqua valley to establish a mission. He decided against it when he found the ranks of the once-proud Umpqua nation decimated by white man's diseases. He wrote that the remaining Indians were "...scattered, degraded and cruel. They are evidently dying away, and as a people without hope and without remedy. Though a mission might save individuals, as a people the Umpquas cannot be saved.... They are darkly, terribly, certainly doomed."

In September 1853 a treaty was signed with the remaining members of the Cow Creek band of the Umpquas. They relinquished their claim to the Umpqua valley in exchange for $12,000 worth of food and supplies and a small reservation. Three years later, in the dead of winter, the Indians were marched north to the Grand Ronde reservation. An eyewitness, homesteader Mary Huntley, gave an account of the day the Indians were forced to leave.

She wrote: "The Indians made the valley ring with the same funeral chant that they made over their dead. It was something terrific, that last howling that the Indians ever made in the Umpqua. It rang out in the crisp morning air that sad day. The march was terrible to them, leaving the homes that had been theirs through all time...."

Of the 300 members of the tribe who marched through the mountains that terrible winter, fewer than 200 survived the Umpqua "Trail of Tears".

COLEY BALL

Coley Ball was a giant. A member of the Klamath tribe, he stood 6'10" and weighed over 300 pounds.

Coley had a cabin built among the willows at the south end of the Wood river valley. He hunted, trapped, and fished. Often he was observed with willow boughs sticking from under his hat or tucked in his belt. The boughs broke his silhouette and made it easier for him to sneak up on wild game.

He ate venison by the quarter and fish by the basketful. His favorite food was eggs. He robbed the wild duck nests and never cared what age or state of hatching the eggs happened to be, claiming, "What difference it make? Egg have shell. Nothing get in."

The Wood river valley became settled and a cream factory was opened at Fort Klamath. Coley visited the creamery asking for hand-outs. One time the crew weighed Coley before and after he gorged himself on buttermilk and discovered the big Indian had gained fifteen pounds.

Coley was a regular visitor to the creamery. Rarely did he walk. Usually he rode a swayback pony and his feet dragged the ground. When they came to a hill Coley, still straddling the animal, would walk his own weight up the grade.

In life Coley never allowed his size to interfere. But in death he presented quite a problem. He was too big to bury in a normal plot. This obstacle was overcome when two plots, end to end, were arranged for his remains in Hill Cemetery overlooking the magnificent Wood river valley.

WALK SITTING DOWN

Long Feathers was one of the first of his race to become civilized. Not long after the white man came to the Oregon Country, Long Feathers joined him and moved to town.

One of the Indian's favorite pastimes was to sit cross-legged at the blacksmith shop, blanket wrapped around his shoulders, intently watching the smithy work the bellows. He was transfixed by the roaring fire and the way the innovative smithy fabricated metal parts for wagons and farm implements, and the way he was able to fit a shoe on even the most stubborn horse.

Long Feathers was a regular fixture all winter. When work was scarce the smithy dug out a pattern and began building a strange contraption from chunks of metal and spare parts. Long Feathers watched as slowly, over the course of several weeks, the smithy built a bicycle. The wheels were made from wagon wheels cut down in size and altered to make them lighter. The seat was fashioned from a number of interlocking horse shoes.

When the project was finally completed the blacksmith wheeled it outside for a test run. He pushed off, pedaled the length of main street, made a big circle and returned to his shop.

Long Feathers was waiting. He took a thoughtful series of puffs on his pipe, blew away the smoke and addressed the blacksmith, "Hmph! White man plenty smart. Him find way walk sitting down."

RAINBOW OBSIDIAN

An Indian woman was drying salmon over a smoky fire when she spotted Yellowjacket stealing fish. She gave chase but Yellowjacket turned and bit her. She died instantly.

The chief of the tribe called council with all the animals of the world. They were asked if they could find the home of Yellowjacket so that he could be punished. No one could. And then Turtle came forward and said he could find Yellowjacket. The Indians laughed at him. How could anything as slow as Turtle ever find Yellowjacket?

The chief raised his hand, called for quiet and said Turtle would be given a chance. Two winters passed before Turtle returned and announced he had discovered the home of Yellowjacket. That night a great feast was held and in the morning the warriors started across the high desert to where Turtle claimed Yellowjacket would be found.

They located the two distinctive hills where Yellowjacket made his home. The warriors decided to set fire to the sagebrush and for two days the fire burned. Then a storm brought rain. As the cloud passed over and the sun reappeared, a beautiful rainbow arced across the sky. It ended at a spot on the south side of one of the hills. The colors were so intense they appeared to continue into the rocky dome. As the afternoon sun slowly slid below a distant line of hills, the rainbow faded.

The Indians raced forward, discovered the Great Spirit had transformed the worthless rock marking the entrance to Yellowjacket's home to obsidian. Obsidian to be used for arrowheads and spear points. Obsidian distinctively marked with the colors of the rainbow.

TRADING

The basalt bench above Celilo Falls was a favorite meeting place for the Indian. The annual gatherings drew tribes from all of the Oregon Country. Columbia River trade goods have been traced as far away as Alaska, southern California and Missouri.

Trade fairs involved more than trading; there were dances, religious ceremonies, races, games and gambling matches. The members of the various tribes had an opportunity to socialize and to share experiences and ideas. Marriages were made and babies were born at trade fairs. It was one event of the year everyone looked forward to attending.

Trade items varied: whale and seal bone and ornamental shells from the coast, obsidian from the Great Basin, and deer and buffalo hides from the plateau region. There was lively trade in food with tribes from each area trading their own specialty: wappato, camas, acorns, bitterroot.

The two products in greatest demand were salmon and slaves. Tribes living along the Columbia River and its tributaries were able to trade smoked salmon to those tribes with poor fishing resources. Slaves were obtained through trade with other tribes or captured in raids. Slaves from faraway places were most prized since it reduced the chance they would try to return home.

Fur traders introduced the Indians to European and American goods: glass beads, wood blankets, brass kettles, iron pots, knives and guns. The unscrupulous among them plied the Indians with alcohol. Alcohol was completely unknown before the coming of the white man. It made a few traders wealthy but it undermined the traditional Indian culture.

THE GOLD POCKET WATCH

The young Siuslaw woman was on hand the day three white men were captured and led into her village.

Council was called; the three men stood trial and it was judged they must die to atone for crimes committed by white men in the past. Their punishment was to be burned at the stake.

Years later one of the men, a fellow named Summers, recalled the events that transpired: "A young squaw, a pretty girl, came around and peered at me. It was with the greatest difficulty, for I was bound to a tree with a leather thong, that I was able to work my hand into my trouser pocket. I had a few trinkets and I dropped them onto the ground one at a time. She picked them up.

"I had nothing more to give. Then I hit upon the idea of enticing her with my pocket watch. I worked it free, held it by the chain and dangled it there in front of her eyes while telling her in Indian jargon that if she helped me escape, the pocket watch would be hers.

"She departed without the slightest hint she would come to my aid. But later, after dark, I felt someone cutting the thong that bound my hands. It was the girl. And after she had freed me, I cut loose my two companions. Before we escaped I kept my promise, giving my watch to the girl and promising her I would return one day.

"After I was safely away I never had cause to travel near the Indian village again, until years later. It was when I was about to ford the Umpqua River at the Reedsport crossing that I happened to notice an Indian woman holding my gold pocket watch. She was the one who had saved me. And in the end I made this faithful woman my wife."

43

PAINT ROCK

It was a plain red rock. The only reason R.S. Jewett, a Rogue River ferryman, had hung onto it was because an old Indian friend had given it to him. He thought it worthless until an assayer happened to see it, ran a few tests and determined it was cinnabar -- the richest piece of ore ever found in the Northwest.

Jewett visited his friend and asked where he had located the red rock. The old Indian told a story of how, many years before, on the eve of a raid planned by the Rogue River Indians against their rivals, the Klamaths, one of the braves discovered a ledge of bright red rock.

The war party moved their camp near the ledge and set about grinding the rock and rubbing the powder on their bodies. Within a few hours they all were sick, gums bleeding and muscles racked with convulsions.

A Klamath slave, seeing his captors in misery, escaped and returned with a hundred Klamath warriors. They were poised to attack the camp of the Rogues when they were driven away by another band of Indians friendly with the Rogues.

In time the majority of the Rogue Indians recovered from their mercury poisoning. The Shaman put a curse that would bring death to anyone who ever revealed the location of the cinnabar ledge.

In the ensuing years several strikes of cinnabar have been made in the Rogue river country but none have come close to the 70% purity of Jewett's sample. The source remains undetected and, according to Indian legend, a death curse guards it for eternity.

44

FLATHEAD

Some Indians living along the Columbia River practiced the custom of flattening the heads of their infants. They strapped their young in papoose carriers and tightened leather straps around the malleable bones of their babies' skulls. The perfect head was to resemble a fat cigar pointed at the chin and the extreme back of the head.

Early trappers, missionaries and pioneers were shocked at the sight of this strange practice. But the world remained ignorant until artist Paul Kane visited the Oregon Country in 1845. He induced an Indian woman, Cow-Wacham, to pose while he painted a profile of her holding her papoose in the process of having its small head flattened.

Kane returned to England and his painting of Cow-Wacham and her child was reproduced in a book, *Wanderings of An Artist Among the Indians of North America*. The civilized world was outraged. Missionaries were sent to the Columbia to persuade the natives to refrain from misshaping heads which God created.

A year after the book was published, Kane returned to the Oregon Country. He stopped at Cow-Wacham's village and was met by a half-breed unfamiliar with the artist. He told Kane that Cow-Wacham was dead, that she had died because her likeness had been transferred to canvas and it had killed her soul. Kane hastily departed.

The practice of flattening heads gradually declined. In 1912 Chief Scoocoom was asked why the custom had ceased and he replied, "Flattening head take much patience. Mothers too lazy these days."

POISON BOTTLE

1847. Disease ravaged the Indian population. The Indians believed the white man was poisoning them in order to steal their land.

At the Whitman Mission, located on the bank of Walla Walla River, Doctor Marcus Whitman treated the Indians. He dispensed medicine and advised them to refrain from their normal remedy of taking sweat baths and jumping in the cold river.

The Cayuse tribe devised a test of the white medicine man. They brought an old man sick with measles to Doctor Whitman. According to the Indian side of the story, if the doctor had been able to cure this man, the massacre at the mission would have been averted.

The doctor administered to the man. But during the night his condition deteriorated. The sun rose. The Indian died.

His death provided sufficient proof to the superstitious Indians. They went on the warpath, killing Doctor Whitman, his wife and twelve others. While the massacre raged, one of the Indians, on a swift horse, carried Doctor Whitman's medicine bottle far away and buried it in the sand near the Columbia River.

CARELESS ACT OF KILLING

Two men, McNall and Findley, grazed horses on the wild grasses of the Wallowa Valley. One day several of their stock came up missing and the pair all too quickly concluded the Nez Perce Indians were to blame.

They rode to the Indian camp, found it occupied by women, children and a few old men. The others were away, carrying in deer killed the previous day. Not expecting trouble they had left their weapons in camp.

When the hunters returned they found McNall and Findley in possession of their bows and rifles. One of the Indians became enraged and grabbed at the weapon in McNall's hands. McNall was stronger. He wrestled the rifle free and shoved the Indian to the ground.

The Indian struggled to his feet and came at McNall. "Shoot!" McNall direct Findley. Findley's rifle jumped, blew a puff of white smoke and the Indian was kicked over backwards.

The two white men turned themselves over to Judge Brainard in Union. They stood trial for the killing of the Indian but it was judged that their actions were in self defense.

A year later the Nez Perce went on the warpath.

JUSTICE

A party of miners was murdered on the flank of Mt. Pitt. Those in the settlement of Jacksonville figured the guilty had to be Klamath Indians and sent a messenger to Chief La Lakes demanding the killers be surrendered.

A special envoy was dispatched from the white settlement to take custody of the guilty. La Lakes met the group in front of his lodge and told them, "Tell your chief, La Lakes punish guilty."

"You must deliver them. They must pay. It is written in the great book," spoke the leader of the group.

"Go," directed La Lakes. "La Lakes, chief of Klamaths. Three sun pass. La Lakes speak."

The miners returned to Jacksonville and on the third day four Klamaths appeared dressed in buckskin bedecked with feathers and beads, red cloth braided in their hair, faces daubed with paint. They carried something wrapped in a blanket tied to two poles.

The miners gathered and one said, "That old Indian sent us a gift. Now, ain't that nice."

"If he thinks he can bribe us...," said another. "An eye for an eye."

The braves stopped and stood for a long moment. Without apparent signal they simultaneously lowered the poles to the ground and stepped back. Three human heads were exposed.

"La Lakes keep word," spoke one of the braves and the Indians departed.

48

INDIAN FIGHTER

Jesse Lewis was a veteran of the Indian wars. On Sundays the white-haired gentleman led the boys' study group at the Cottage Grove Methodist Church.

It was his habit to begin by asking, "You boys learn the lesson for today?"

The boys would nod and one of their hands would shoot up. Jesse would nod toward the boy and the youngster, excitement showing through, would ask, "Sir, we was hopin' maybe you would tell us about the time you found the buried Indian."

Jesse would reach for his pocket watch, squint at the time. "Well now, I reckon since you boys know your lesson we could squeeze in a story." He would roll his shoulders, massage away the years, sit a little straighter and begin.

"I was with a group of soldiers and we was chasin' a whole tribe of Injuns. Came across this mound of sand and I thought somethin' seemed peculiar. Went to pokin' 'round and pretty soon this squaw raised up with a papoose in her arms.

"Wasn't much sense messin' with the squaw. Rolled her back in the grave, but nobody was up to killing a baby so took him with us, back to the fort. We raised 'im. First words that kid spoke was cuss words 'cause the soldiers were a pretty rough lot. Not like you boys...."

After several more stories Jesse would again remove his pocket watch and exclaim, "Oh my, time sure flies. Class dismissed. Read your lesson. We'll go over it next Sunday."

SIGNS OF A STRUGGLE

The fall of 1893 a sheepherder from Pendleton came across a ghastly scene in the bottom of Dark Canyon.

According to the sign, an Indian woman had been picking huckleberries. Evidently she had placed her papoose in a shady spot while she wandered the hillside collecting plump berries. Her papoose must have screamed because the basket had been dropped. Berries were scattered on the ground.

A grizzly was dragging away the papoose; the Indian woman flew at the bear. The animal, protecting its meal, turned on her. She unsheathed her knife, stabbed at the bear, drew blood. The bear bellowed in rage and took a powerful swipe at its tormentor, sending the woman hurtling fully twenty feet through the air. She lay where she landed, trying to gather her senses, bleeding into the soft earth.

The bear must have returned his attention to the papoose. The baby cried and the woman was on her feet. She charged, lashed at the bear with her knife. The beast knocked her back, but again and again she attacked. Finally, bleeding heavily, the woman no longer possessed the strength to rise.

The sheepherder walked around examining the mute evidence. He dug a grave and buried the baby in her mother's arms. And then he picked up his rifle and went hunting the bear.

ESCAPE

Bill Stillwell volunteered to fight the Indians in the Cayuse Indian War of 1848. He was made a field scout.

One day he was riding ahead of the main detachment, scouting for sign near Emigrant Springs in the Blue Mountains, when he spotted a band of Indians and gave chase. He later told what happened.

"Before I realized what I was doing I had chased those redskins right back to their camp. I was surrounded. Arrows were whistling around me. Only chance I had was to lay flat against my horse's neck and let him have his head. But he stumbled, went down. I jumped clear and ran. An Indian passed me, sent an arrow into my hip. I fell, jumped up, broke the arrow off and scrambled over the rocks and dodged through the sage. I went where a horse couldn't go.

"I was bleeding pretty bad and my strength was starting to go before I found a hiding spot and holed up. I could hear the Indians all around searching for me. Finally the sun went down and at last I figured I might have a ghost of a chance of getting away."

Under the cover of darkness Bill crawled and limped back to the trail and at daybreak he came across an Indian pony. By then he was too stoved up from his hip wound to mount. He led the horse over to a boulder and with great difficulty crawled onto the horse's back.

"It wasn't until the following morning that I made camp," recalled Bill. "One of the men spotted me and yelled, 'It's Bill Stillwell! He ain't dead!'

"But ever since then I've carried a reminder, got a flint arrowhead embedded in my hip. Doctor says he can't operate, that I'll pack it to my grave."

LONG RIDE

The Yakima Indians went on the warpath and news of the uprising was sent east with express rider W.H. Pearson. He departed The Dalles and rode all day and night to reach McKay's ranch on the Umatilla River. No one was home at the ranch so Pearson helped himself to a saddle horse.

As he swung into the saddle a war whoop cut the air. From a draw came a wave of mounted Indians. Pearson dug his spurs into the fresh mount and raced across the flat with the Indians in hot pursuit.

Once he had outdistanced the Indians, Pearson swung off the main trail and set a course parallel to it. He traveled that way, avoiding danger, until he reached the mission at Lapwai, Idaho.

After a short rest, and with an Indian guide leading the way, Pearson started into the Bitterroot mountain range. They were overtaken by a storm with high winds and heavy snow. The Indian was breaking trail when, without warning, the wind uprooted a tree and it fell, killing both the guide and his horse.

Pearson continued. The snow became deeper and at last the horse quit. Pearson fashioned snowshoes from willow branches and struggled onward and upward. After four days he crossed the mountains and reached the Bitterroot valley where he secured a new horse. He rode three more days to reach Fort Benton.

He arrived so cold and exhausted that he had to be helped off the horse. His ride across 650 miles of desolate country, to alert the world that the Yakima Indians were on the warpath, was one of the most remarkable chapters in the history of the West.

COAT-OF-MANY-COLORS

One winter the storekeeper at Grand Ronde, the center of the Oregon coastal reservation, received a shipment of unique overcoats. They were made of gaudy horse blankets and were popular, even prized, by the local population.

Charley, a tall, lean Indian, wanted one of the coats, wanted one very badly; but he did not have the means and was forced to watch as others came, paid the price and departed. The pile of coats dwindled.

At last Charley concluded he would have to work in order to purchase one of the coats. He contracted with a white settler to supply split rails. When he had earned enough money he returned to the store.

By then only one coat, a small size, remained. He paid for the coat and pulled it on. The sleeves hit him just below the elbow. But as he stood on the boardwalk in front of the store admiring his reflection in the window, he was smiling broadly and seemed well pleased with himself.

Then it began to rain. The rain came hard, driven by a strong wind. The storekeeper watched Charley strip off his coat, shirt and trousers. He wrapped the coat protectively inside the shirt and trousers and, naked except for moccasins and a shapeless felt hat, he ran toward his cabin.

LIFTING SCALPS

W. A. Van Gothem was a pioneer, a cowboy, and a man who was scalped by Indians and lived to tell about it.

He was looking for cattle with a friend on the high desert bordering Snake River. They had dropped to the river and were about to cross when a wild whoop split the air. A war party of mounted Indians swooped over the hill. The white men dug spurs into their mounts and charged into the river. Van Gothem was wounded and fell in the water; his partner was killed.

The Indians drug the bodies ashore, proceeded to lift the scalp of the dead man and were in the process of taking Van Gothem's when a priest in a flowing black robe suddenly appeared. The Indians were very surprised. Thinking this surely must be a spirit they leaped on their horses and galloped away.

The priest quickly went to the aid of his fellow men. He found Van Gothem was still breathing. He cleaned the head wound and managed to slow the bleeding. For a number of days he stayed with Van Gothem and eventually the wounded man regained his strength.

A man with a weaker constitution might have given up but not Van Gothem. In later years, rather than allowing his terrible scar around the top of his head to be an impairment, he wore it as a badge. He lived into his 80s and passed away in his sleep in McMinnville, Oregon.

MOTHER

The Scott family homesteaded along the lower Burnt River. During the three years they were there two children were born, a boy and a girl.

Then came an afternoon when, like the sweep of a hand, the young family was destroyed. On that day the Scotts were returning to the homestead with a wagonload of supplies. They had just entered a narrow spot when a bloodcurdling whoop and rifle shots erupted from both sides of the road.

Mr. Scott immediately pitched forward, dropping the reins and starting over the wagon dash. But Mrs. Scott, with strength she never knew she possessed, pulled him back onto the seat. The horses were running wild. Indians were shooting. Babies were crying. The reins were bouncing along on the ground.

Mrs. Scott reacted. She crawled over the dash, stepped on-to the tongue, grabbed one rein and then the other. She returned to the wagon seat, pulled on the reins and slowly began to regain control. She was able to stop the team at the neighbor's place and informed him, "My husband is dead. I have been hit, too."

With that she lost her balance, fell onto the ground and lay bleeding. She whispered instructions, "Send the children to my parents." And then she requested to see her children. She kissed the boy, then the girl.

Mr. and Mrs. Scott were buried in each other's arms.

FISHING

The salmon was as important to the Indians of the Oregon Country as the buffalo was to the Plains Indians. The return each spring of the salmon marked the beginning of the fishing season. Large villages were established along major rivers. It was a time of plenty with fish being cured for periods when Mother Nature would not be so generous.

Rapids and waterfalls slowed the runs of fish. Here, above the white water, Indians built wooden platforms by lashing planking and poles together and used long-handled dipnets or spears to harvest the salmon. In smaller, slower streams Indians constructed rock, log or brush weirs that directed the salmon into a basket trap or a shallow pool where they could easily be speared.

The men did the fishing while the women tended the catch. They split the salmon and laid the halves to sun dry or to cure over a slow-burning, smoky fire. The preserved salmon could be used for food or as a trade item.

In addition to salmon the Indians of the Oregon Country fished for steelhead, mullet, suckers, trout and sturgeon. Along the coast and lower Columbia, Indians were able to dipnet large numbers of smelt. Inland, they fished with hook and line. Hooks were made of wood, stone or bone. Line was manufactured from plant fibers or by cutting thin leather strips. When the fish were not biting, the Indians threw poisonous plants into pools to stupify the fish and assure a good catch.

GREAT SPIRIT SPEAKS

The Oregon Country belonged to the Indian. So it was for countless centuries. And then rumors circulated of a new breed; men with white skin, light hair and bushy beards who lived on the far side of the mountains, across the Great Plains.

The white man came, traders, trappers, miners and pioneers. Government men were sent to meet with the Indians, to persuade them to sign treaties relinquishing all claim to the land. The white man offered trinkets, blankets, knives and guns.

But the white men were told, "We have arrow. Will it not kill? We have obsidian. Will it not cut? Indian have no use for fire stick, for knife. See this robe? It buffalo, it keep me warm in winter. No need blanket.

"Great Spirit provide for Indian. Give food. Give us way kill. Give us fire. We need no more. You go back where you come. We not want your gifts. We want to keep our land."

But the white man continued to flood the country, taking control of the land and forcing the Indian onto reservations. The buffalo were killed. The rivers were dammed and the salmon stopped running. The virgin soil was tilled, roads built, cities created. All this has come to pass in a few short generations.

The Indian warns, "The Great Spirit is not pleased with the white man. You will see."